Red Wool Socks and Dark Chocolate:
A Life in Three Lines

SHORT VERSE POEMS
by
Marti Keller

Matrika Press
Publisher

Red Wool Socks and Dark Chocolate: A Life in Three Lines
Copyright © Marti Keller
May 2020

All Rights Reserved
including the right of reproduction,
copying, or storage in any form
or means, including electronic,
In Whole or Part,
without prior written
permission of the author.

ISBN: 978-1-946088-21-5

1. Poetry 2. Haiku 3. Title

Matrika Press

Matrika Press
P.O. Box 115
Rockwood, Maine 04478
Editor@MatrikaPress.com

www.MatrikaPress.com

Dedication

My fond thoughts return frequently to a group of women who met up to write and read poetry over many years in Berkeley California. We called ourselves Shakespeare's Sisters, after the question asked by English writer Virginia Woolf about what if the Bard had "an equally gifted sister" whose writing was taken seriously, whose work was performed and published in her time.

We were young mothers, somewhat older mothers, therapists, school counselors, journalists, yo-yo champions. We gathered in coffee shops and in houses. We encouraged each other to submit our poems to the myriad small presses edited by women, and to read our work in public settings.

More than a half century later, I am still waking up to my own voice, in no small part due to their encouragement, critique, and friendship.

And the gifts they shared.

1

can't have too many red wool socks
or dark chocolate bars
any given January

on this New Year's Day
should clean each orange blind slat
count the years of shade

collard green shortage
small enough deprivation
this year, magnified

a few days past the New Year
giant glass balls on bare oak branches
bird cacophony like spring

otter sighting
around the corner
dashing for the sewaged creek

he loved the flashy male cardinals
toward the end, he could only say
red bird

no other lights on
never noticed before
we are the first to rise

become mismatched
socks, tops, bottoms
block, town, country

double forgetting
now, between the two of us
can't find our spices

keep looking for signs
watching the green bananas
refuse to ripen

the young dogwood would not put forth
 even a few orange leaves
perhaps, then, spring blossoms

due to this aging
can no longer shed tears
but still touch my toes

two speeding mail trucks
swerve past each other
deadly deliveries

on Monday mornings
never read the obits
knowing: there is death

an ancient remedy
might there be a tiger balm
that cures cosmic pain

morning shower
confession to spouse--
rescued a spider

where rented goats
grazed on remnant December grasses
January daffodils

Scotch broom is for March
not mid-winter
before killing snow

in this crazier climate
hard to tell
chirping birds—or crickets

reading through back papers
I forget
to skip the horoscope

if it's going to be this gloomy
this kind of pewter gray
a downpour would seem reasonable

woke up still invisible
except to three waiting dogs
wanting out of crates, fed.

every morning poems
by the time it is light
the day has flattened

Atlanta surprise
a quart of radish kimchee
from the Vietnamese bakery

when there is only lettuce to pick
each head
is lovely

more reports of blossom spotting
a February spring
time to shake out the winter mat

all the daffodils
especially the feral ones
come up the same time

perplexing
the loveliest dogwoods
grow in abandoned yards

8

frozen earthworms
another reason to loathe
the turn back to winter

out the window
a trickster sun
thirty seven degree wind chill

on the constructed lake
in a once restricted town
the ducks and geese glide separately

at exactly seven
another round of raining
Saturday in ruins

so glad for company
when the dining room table
has been lemon oiled

today's freeway gridlock
40,000 pounds
of spilled Georgia greens

another morning
no new words for rain pounding
metaphors drowning

in an otherwise
chaotic office
mostly sorted paper clips

on the same street
one yard, cherry blossoms
another, fallen leaves

it's one thing to realize
you have too many forks
another, too little company

dearest neighbors
put down your rakes and blowers
await mulched magic

fallen sticks, grasses
make for a disorderly yard
but happy monarchs

drabbed yellow leaf show
is it nature's lottery
or my dulled vision?

swollen right toe
the Midwest rivers as well
we all need sun, warmth

he fills a gym bag
with swim suit, google
I fill a floor bucket

my son brings me soap
mango, rejuvenating
like he is, always

I rarely bake/broil
one houseplant remains
choose instead, dancing

as punishment
the rose I stole yesterday
withered overnight

such a bland
morning sky
such a pink sunset

morning sounds
a song bird, the refrigerator
points of concentration

geographic craves
used to be first artichokes
now Vidalias

over-eager gardeners
should leave be
dandelions, violets, clover

small luxury
bagged organic English pears
six dollars apiece

rabbit sightings
babies birthed in tall grasses
mowed down tragedies

after the senate vote
downed branches
tornado winds

real snow flurries
feckless cherry trees
rooting for the blossoms

sound of aging
the shuffle, shuffle
of protective slippers

must discard
year-old matzo meal
electoral funk

flood soaked Midwest states
brace for blinding blizzards
I store winter clothes

another southern portent
crocus shoots
poking through cold mud

purple redbuds
belie the drab persistence
of stark bare branches

16

seed hogging
red winged blackbirds
merit: graciousness in flight

week old cut flowers
two dollars a bunch
adequate beauty

why the need to find out
where storms comes from-
they're here

a pause in thunder
like a holiday cease fire
song birds caroling

sometimes just cleaning
twelve panes on a front door
makes for a full day

the Methodists
with their pious yard
their one pink flamingo

like vintage bathtubs
can we elder people
be repaired, restored, reglazed

reasons to stay here
long-buried ancient mosses
unearthed, faithful

half-finished bouquet
from the bargain flower bin
needs ferns

rushed Saturday morning
a run through farmers market
peaches less sweet

two old dogs
under the kitchen table
truce

trapped by smashed toe
must wait
for an onion

Halloween
our town is costumed
in damp leaves

nearly missed the fall
then an acorn fell
and I didn't

autumn skipped over
no time to mourn
buy a winter pear

extraverts'
monastery
a day of air travel

rain sounds all night
the deepest sleep
in forever

training our nature
to look wild
takes daily work

when my mother
ran out of money
she mailed me red wool socks

A Life in Three Lines | Marti Keller

About the Author

Marti Keller began writing haiku, like many of us, in middle school, as part of a creative writing curriculum – with its insistence on three line 5-7-5 syllable structure and the natural world.

She is grateful for the opportunity to have attended a North America haiku conference. There she gained new insights and marvelous examples of more culturally appropriate, expansive approaches to how these brief, immediate verses, which originated in Japan, have been embraced and adapted across world cultures.

She now writes these momentary observations and reflections with attention to objects and experiences in one's everyday life, and with a structure that acknowledges and values diverse expression.

Marti's poetry has been published in weekly and monthly magazines, in collections focused on women's writing, in Unitarian Universalist meditation books and other forums.

She has published several chapbooks, including *Thinking in Haiku*, *Prickly Pear*, and *South/West*.

www. revmartikeller.com
www.MatrikaPress.com/marti-keller

About the Publisher

Matrika Press is an independent publishing house dedicated to publishing works in alignment with liberal religious Values and Principles. Its fiscal sponsor is Unitarian Universalist Women and Religion, a 501c3 organization.

Matrika Press publishes anthologies, memoirs, poetry, prayer and ritual manuscripts, and other books to bring meaning and transformation to the world. A primary goal of Matrika Press is to publish stories and works that would otherwise remain untold. We also resurrect out-of-print manuscripts to ensure our historical works remain accessible.

Why the name "Matrika"?
It is said that Matrika is the intrinsic energy or sound vibration of the 50 letters of the Sanskrit alphabet called "the mothers of creation." The Goddess Kali Ma used the letters to form words, and from the words formed all things. This aligns with scriptures that assert "in the beginning was the Word," and in other sacred texts that affirm people of all backgrounds and faiths agree: Words are powerful. More than that: Their vibrations are creative forces; they bring all things into being.

Matrika Press titles are automatically made available to tens of thousands of retailers, libraries, schools, and other distribution and fulfillment partners, including Amazon, Barnes & Noble, Chapters/Indigo (Canada), and other well-known book retailers and wholesalers across North America, and in the United Kingdom, Europe, Australia and New Zealand and other Global partners.

For more information, visit:

www.MatrikaPress.com

Other Books by Matrika Press

www.MatrikaPress.com

www.MatrikaPress.com

Featured Titles

Where the Sky has No Stars is the first published collection of Wesley Burton's poetry. His poems reflect his deep appreciation for Nature and keen intuitions on the human experience. Contemplative and imaginative, his poetry entices readers to face moments of transition. His work explores the inner depths of the psyche, the healing power of Nature, and the soul's resilience to move forward out of darkness.

Wesley's desire to share this work with others in the hope that his words may help those faced with similar challenges demonstrates deep compassion.

www.MatrikaPress.com/where-the-sky-has-no-stars

JT Curran's poetry blends colorful observations with thought-provoking reflections. As both poet and musician, he draws upon influences from the Beat Generation: Kerouac, Ginsberg, Burroughs and Snyder. In all, **Beyond the Road** weaves a journey through time covering more than five decades.

With wit, compassion, irony, and humor, this book invites the reader to consider the signposts, off-ramps, co-travelers and vistas which populate our journeys. JT's words remind us that however we may navigate our experiences, our destination remains beyond the road.

www.MatrikaPress.com/beyond-the-road

Sue Roy Humphries' historic aggregation work featuring behind-the-scenes documentation of sci-fi and horror classics in theatrical make-up effects has been all but hidden from the world for decades. Originally published in 1980, **Making a Monster** has been long out of print.

Matrika Press is delighted to revive this manuscript on its 40th Anniversary in response to those seeking a comprehensive montage of this highly creative aspect of filmmaking.

Making a Monster reveals the artistic secrets of your favorite vintage fantasy films. This book is filled with detailed accounts of the early era of makeup processes and ingenious solutions to the challenges of pre-CGI Visual FX.

While the manuscript reveals the trade and techniques of transforming some of Hollywood's most beautiful and beloved icons into infamous villains and fantastical creatures, its content also lends a lens unto the human psyche, including that of choosing what to believe in. Said another way, choosing One's Faith.

www.MatrikaPress.com/making-a-monster

The **Circle Model of Shared Leadership** by Elizabeth Fisher is a concrete group facilitation process that balances achieving tasks with emotional bonding. By using this book you will:

- Learn ways to bring a collection of individuals together, in a committee, board, or activist project, uniting each one's efforts which are equally valued.

- Develop skills critical to honing participatory decision-making and supporting the soul of the group, which must be kept strong if the group is to accomplish its goals.

- Discover important principles, practices and tools that support effective collaboration within and among all the levels of organizations.

Elizabeth has been a leader in the UU Women & Religion movement since the early 1980s. She is the author of the participatory course *Rise Up and Call Her Name: A Woman-honoring Journey into Global Earth-based Spiritualities* originally published by the Unitarian Universalist Women's Federation.

www.MatrikaPress.com/the-circle-model

www.MatrikaPress.com

www.ingramcontent.com/pod-product-compliance
Lightning Source LLC
Chambersburg PA
CBHW052129110526
44592CB00013B/1808